ACKNOWLEDGEMENT

To my children: BSW, MSW, and MASW.

Choose your careers by pursuing what you love.

ABOUT THE AUTHOR

Michael A. Wright is Chairman of MAWMedia Group, LLC. in Nashville, TN. A former BSW & MSW Social Work program director, Wright has taught a diverse population of students at both the baccalaureate and master degree levels. His other research interests include trauma and resilience, complex adaptive systems, and entrepreneurship.

Succeed @ www.mawmedia.com

i

Introduction to Social Work:

A Writing Approach to Professional Discovery

By Michael A. Wright, PhD, LAPSW

mawmedia Group

Nashville TN

Introduction to Social Work: A Writing Approach to Professional Discovery / By Michael A. Wright, PhD, LAPSW

ISBN: 978-0-9842170-7-6

Publisher: MAWMedia Group

First Edition: November 2015

Cover photo courtesy of anakkml posted on freedigitalphotos.net

Table of Contents

For Writing Assignments: Hegelian Dialectic

Writing assignments are to be formatted using the writing logic model called the Hegelian Dialectic. The writing logic model employs a three-part presentation pattern. The writing assignment begins with the thesis. The thesis is followed by the antithesis. The synthesis completes the writing logic and the presentation.

The first part presents a **thesis**. The thesis states the primary position the paper is meant to argue. In addition to a statement of thesis, supporting evidence in the form of factual data may be written. Anecdotal evidence may also be used to illustrate certain ideas, but should always be supported with aggregate data demonstrating that the anecdote is one of many possible examples.

The second part presents an **antithesis**. The antithesis is a contradiction of the thesis or an alternative assertion to the thesis. This contradiction responds to each point presented in the thesis presentation with an evidence or data-based argument. Care is taken to respond to the assertions of fact made by the thesis toward the construction of an alternative point of view.

The third and final part in this writing logic model presents a **synthesis**. The synthesis is a reconciliation of the thesis and antithesis. The synthesis works to explain how both the thesis and antithesis can exist together even while in opposition to one another. Typically, this is achieved through the presentation of new information or identifying commonalities within the thesis and antithesis that were not highlighted in the prior presentations.

The goal of this writing logic model is to formulate and communicate reason in writing. Writing assignments utilizing this writing logic model can be judged on a 3 point scale. Evaluators may identify each of the required parts logging a point for each part presented. Poor grammar and spelling may be noted and corrected, but not judged in the point evaluation.

Hegelian Dialectic Essay Grading Rubric

Perfect +3	Adequate +2	Marginal +1	Zero +0
Thesis is a statement, antithesis contradicts the thesis, and synthesis resolves the conflict. Also sections are formatted obviously in separate paragraphs or with headings.	Writing assignment has 3 sections, but they are not specified with new paragraph formatting or headings.	Writing assignment has 3 sections but conflicting points of view or resolution of conflict is missing	Writing assignment was attempted with no sections or discussion of multiple points of view.

[WRITING EXAMPLE] Expectation of Success

I expect success from every student in the course. Success means that you are engaged in a decision about whether the profession of social work is right for you. A career in Social Work may not be right for everyone. My goal is to ensure that your decision is an informed one.

Many students are more concerned with a passing final grade. This preoccupation sometimes causes disconnect between the goals of a professor and the goals of a student. Instructional design can assist the professor in engaging the student, supporting productivity, and making learning fun. With instruction that engages the student, a student can find her interest represented in the content while the professor motivates reflectiveness. Instruction that supports productivity provides examples of excellence that a student can pattern his work after while the professor encourages successes. Instruction can make learning fun through games while the professor incorporates repetition of concepts.

It is possible for the goals of the student to coexist with the goals of the professor. Achievement of competency in the concepts presented will result in an acceptable grade. No matter what career choice you eventually pursue, the content presented here will ensure that you know what the profession of social work is all about.

-o-

SECTION I: ORIGINS OF THE SOCIAL WORK PROFESSION

CHAPTER 1

LEARNING ACTIVITIES

Review an introduction to the profession of social work. Reflect on your interest in the profession.

WRITING ASSIGNMENT

Articulate the guiding premise for professional intervention in the social work profession.

Chapter 1: What is Social Work?

What is Social work?

Professional Social Work is rooted in the principles of service, social justice, dignity and worth of the person, the importance of human relationships, integrity, and competence. The profession is characterized by:

- a theoretical basis,
- an identified approach,
- observability,
- political standing,
- practical settings, and
- a code of ethical conduct.

What makes social work different?

Social work interprets systems theory to implement a Person-in-Environment (PIE) perspective. This means that social work assesses both the individual and their surroundings in order to create solutions.

Medical, psychological, and sociological interventions today will integrate biological, psychological, social, and often spiritual considerations that impact behavior and well-being just as social work does. Social work is different because it is the only helping profession that mandates individual and social change as its core practice. A fully integral view of social work would recognize its difference from other professions as a function of its practice including perception of the individual with their environment, creation of a reality through interactive effects, impacting and impacted by institutional policies, and creation a culture that either supports or hinders collective well-being.

How old is social work?

The practice of community helpers can be traced to the early 1900's with the emergence of Charity Organization Societies (COS). Most professionals agree that social work as we know it developed from these roots through 1955 when the National Association of Social Workers (NASW) was created as the national voice of the profession. That makes social work over 60 years old, a relatively young profession.

How many years does it take to complete a social work education?

A Bachelor degree in social work (BSW) or Bachelor of Science in Social Work degree (BSSW) includes liberal arts education and two years of foundation, generalist content. Most BSW programs are mapped for 8 semesters, typically four years.

Master of social work (MSW) degree programs are mapped for 4 semesters, typically two years. For students who successfully complete a BSW program, the MSW degree can be completed in less time—as little as 2 semesters for some social work master degree programs.

PhD programs are usually designated Doctor of Philosophy in Social Work (PhD) or Doctor of Social Work (DSW). Many former DSW programs today only grant the PhD degree. The PhD degree typically requires two years of coursework and a research-based dissertation. The DSW is typically considered a practice degree—a terminal degree for social work practitioners.

What do social workers learn to do?

Social work practice is commonly referred to as generalist at the Bachelor degree level or advanced generalist at the Master degree level. Generalist social work refers to the breath of training for individual and social change across populations of individuals, families, groups, organizations and communities. Advanced generalist social work refers to training in the supervision, administration, and evaluation of workers, interventions, and programs.

What are the essential skills of the social worker?

Social work practice at all levels requires authenticity, empathy, and respect. In work with individuals, authenticity enables genuine relationships and the ability to build trust. Empathy in work with individuals allows the social worker to understand the choices of the client as reasonable. Respect in work with individuals reminds the social worker to inform the choices of the client, but allow the client to make their own choices or self-determine.

Authenticity in work with organizations and communities ensures that the social worker applies principles in practice to create just and equitable policies and environments. Empathy in work with organizations and communities remind social workers to advocate for social and economic justice while promoting communities that they would like to live within. Respect in work with organizations and communities means that social workers listen to indigenous people, respect the sanctity of place, and promote dignity in policy making and policy practice.

What settings do social workers work in?

A wide range of modifiers are applied to Generalist and Advanced Generalist social workers indicating the populations, expertise, or systems levels of practice.

Social workers can be found in medical facilities, government and not-for-profit agencies, corporations, nursing homes, federal and state government, schools, community mental health agencies, churches, and in private practice.

Social casework involves assessing clients and addressing social, health, economic, and child welfare.

Medical social work involves managing the needs of patients and their families including treatment directives, rehabilitation, discharge planning, home-health, and palliative care.

School social work places professionals in educational settings to assist teachers and administrators in creating a learning environment for children who may face economic, emotional, and social challenges.

Clinical social work can be found in counseling centers or corporations providing mental health and psychotherapy services.

Administration and Supervision requires social workers to develop, implement, and evaluate other social workers, social policies, and social welfare programs.

Community Organization utilizes social work systems knowledge to improve the physical and social support environment for clients.

Social Research involves social workers in both inductive inquiry and deductive experiments that analyze the impact of human behavior, social interaction, social policy, and practice models.

What populations do social workers work with?

Social workers work with the range between children and elderly, upper class and underclass, local and international, corporate and individual. Social workers see practice populations as **IFGOC**—individuals, families, groups, organizations, and communities.

What salary can be expected for social workers?

The Bureau of Labor statistics divides social work practice areas into four categories: Child, Family, and School social workers; Health care social workers; and, Mental Health and Substance

Abuse social workers. The median annual wage for all 607,300 social workers in 2012 was $44,200.

- Child, family, and school social workers can expect a median income of $41,530 employing 285,700 workers.
- Health care social workers earn a median income of $49,830 employing 146,200 workers.
- Mental health and substance abuse social workers earn a median income of $39,980 employing 114,200.

The bureau projects that social work workforce will grow by 19 percent leading up to 2022 or faster than the average 11% growth of all occupations. Health care social work will experience the greatest growth increasing 27%. Mental health and substance abuse social workers will increase by 23%.

What licenses are required for social workers?

In most states and provinces, registration is available at all levels of education BSW, MSW and PhD. In each state or province, licensing is administered by a state or provincial social work board.

Most boards distinguish between generalist, advanced generalist, and clinical social workers. A clinical license is available only to professionals who possess a Master degree in social work, have completed two years of post-Master degree, supervised experience, and successfully complete a licensure examination.

Rules and regulations vary by state, but specific questions can be answered by the social work board of your state or province. The Association of Social Work Boards (*ASWB.org*), a national organization, lists contact information for state and provincial governments as well as information about examinations, and other licensing specifics on their website.

Bibliographic Notes

Wage information was verified, 2012 data, with the Bureau of Labor Statistics, bls.gov. The site also reports location quotients, highest concentrations, and annual mean wages by state and metropolitan areas.

Information on social work practice areas and positions was gleaned from *NASWdc.org*.

[WRITING EXAMPLE] The Difference: Individual and Social Change

Social work is different from Psychology and Sociology. Social Work is traditionally presented as an applied behavioral science focused on improving services to the clients. Psychology tends to focus on the exploration of mental processes and influences categorized into social, cognitive, psychoanalytic, developmental, and behavioral sectors. Sociology studies groups and group interaction from the perspective of functionalism, conflict, interactionism, or phenomenology.

Each of the professions is similar in some ways. Each is typically considered a behavioral science. This may be due to the fact that human behavior is a common point of observation in psychology, sociology, and social work. Current explorations in each of the fields recognize the impact of biology, thoughts, relationships, and environment on human behavior.

Social workers historically promoted the idea that the social work profession is the only behavior science to perceive the individual within their environment. This was termed the Person-In-Environment perspective. Psychology, traditionally focused on the individual and his internal thoughts, today includes an awareness of the environment and other influences. Sociology, traditionally concerned primarily with the group reality and environments, today includes awareness of how individual characteristics impact group behavior.

Many similarities exist between the consideration of Social Work, Psychology and Sociology, but Social Work has a distinctive difference from the other professional degrees. Social Work professionals practice individual change and social change. The tandem is a mandate of the profession. No social work professional can be content with only one or the other.

Individual change, at its best, includes attention to the cognitive, behavioral, and sense-making components of human action. Social change includes attention to institutional structures, policies, and evaluation procedures. No other profession holds as its professional mandate to act explicitly for individual change and social change.

-o-

CHAPTER 2

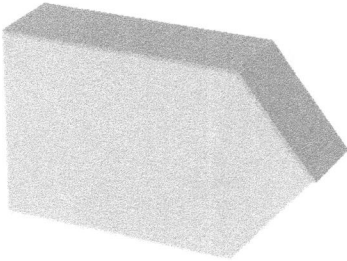

LEARNING ACTIVITIES

List the attributes of a profession. Compare Greenwood (1957) and Flexner (1915).

WRITING ASSIGNMENT

Discuss the contributions of one pioneer or influential personality unique to the social work profession.

Chapter 2: Defining a Profession

FLEXNER AND RICHMOND 1915

Abraham Flexner commented on the professional status of social work in a paper attributed to conference proceedings of the 1915, 42nd annual National Conference on Charities and Corrections. The paper was published by the MacMillan Company in its Saturday, May 8, 1915 edition of "School and Society."

Among other comments in his paper, he stated, "In the long run, the first, main and indispensable criterion of a profession will be the possession of a professional spirit, and that test social work may, if it will, fully satisfy"

Mary Richmond is credited with outlining the definition that was the contemporary response to Flexner. In her 1922 work, she noted that social casework is rooted in an approach to social relationship and personality (Social Casework, 1922, p. 97).

She defines social case work as separate from any specialization in "questions of restoration to self-support, with matters of health and personal hygiene, as well as with the intricacies of mental hygiene" (p. 97).

Social casework, in her definition, "consists of those processes which develop personality through adjustments consciously effected, individual by individual, between men and their social environment" (p. 98-99).

COMPARISON FLEXNER TO GREENWOOD

In 1915, Abraham Flexner listed six attributes of a profession:

1. Professional activity is based on intellectual action along with personal responsibility

2. The practice of a profession is based on knowledge, not routine activities

3. There is practical application rather than just theorizing

4. There are techniques that can be taught

5. A profession is organized internally tending toward association

6. A profession is motivated by altruism, with members working in some sense for the good of society.

In 1957, Ernest Greenwood, after joining the University of California-Berkeley faculty in 1953, wrote an article some credit with securing the legitimacy of the social work profession.

Greenwood listed 5 attributes:

1. Systematic body of theory: general and specific knowledge and understanding that underlie and guide the professional's use of technique.

2. Professional authority: gained from extensive education, knowledge, and use of technique.

3. Community sanction: informal sanction of the profession and professional authority and formal sanction through law or policy.

4. Code of Ethics: a written code ascribed to by professionals.

5. Professional culture: Formal culture like settings and client relationships; informal culture such as values, norms and common symbols.

Flexner's attributes today may be described as Deliberate, Analytical, Practical, Competency-based, Organized Internally, and Altruistic. Greenwood's attributes today may be described as Theoretically Framed, Licensed, Respected, Ethical, and Professional in Culture.

Flexner's	Greenwood's	Comparison
Deliberate	Theoretically Framed	Theoretical Basis
Knowledge-based	Licensed	Evidence-based
Practical	Respected	Politically Viable
Competency-based		Practical Settings
Organized Internally	Professional in Culture	Observable Approach
Altruistic	Ethical	Ethically Governed

From a comparison of these concepts, let us define a set of professional requirements for the profession of social work. The professional requirements may include Theoretical Basis, Evidence-based Approach, Political Viability, Practical Settings, an Observable Approach, and a Code of Ethical Conduct.

It is no mistake that accredited social work programs across the country train students in Human Behavior in the Social Environment, Practice, Policy, Field, Research, and Social Work Values and Ethics.

Comparison	Social Work Education Content
Theoretical Basis	Human Behavior in the Social Environment
Evidence-based	Practice
Politically Viable	Policy
Practical Settings	Field
Observable Approach	Research
Ethically Governed	Social Work Values and Ethics

Bibliographic Notes

The importance of Flexner has been the source of some debate. An interesting paper was published by David M. Austin in the September 1983 issue of Social Service Review. The article questions the value of continuing to use Flexner's criteria for defining the attributes of the social work profession. Write your response to Flexner's critique of the social work profession, especially the line "In the long run, the first, main and indispensable criterion of a profession will be the possession of a professional spirit, and that test social work may, if it will, fully satisfy."

The National Association of Social Workers Foundation maintains a database of social work pioneers at *naswfoundation.org/pioneers/*.

[WRITING EXAMPLE] The Social Work Professional Spirit

More than the populations, academic content, service options, agency structures, and ecological systems social workers operate within, the social work professional spirit may be understood as that something that binds all social workers together. Let us take two approaches to understanding what Flexner meant. The first is an amateur etymology of the word spirit, starting with the word and working backward to find a definition and application to social work. The second approach is to assume that "spirit" refers to a mythological representation connoted by the word.

Definition by Spirit

The word "spirit" finds its origins in the Latin, "spiritus" referring to breath. It may be considered closely related to conceptions of what makes a person alive. As well, similar to conceptions of ghosts, spirit could be considered what is left after the body is gone. Utilizing this etymology, the question, "What is the social work professional spirit?" may be changed to, "What is lingers after a social worker has done her work?"

Could it be that what is left is best expressed in the social work ethical principles? Social workers leave a mark of service, social justice, dignity and worth of the person, the importance of human relationships, integrity, and competence wherever and whenever they intervene. But, Flexner presented the requirement for a code of ethical conduct, so "professional spirit" may be more than just this.

The Soul of Social Work

In Greek mythology, the personification of "spirit" is Psycke. The word is synonymous with "soul." In Greek, the word for soul is also related to the word for life. This interpretation may, in fact, change the question from, "What is the social work professional spirit?" to "What is the life of social worker?"

Could it be that the life of the social worker is one of constant consideration of the individual impact and the social impact? When social workers see life being lived, they see people who make choices, but they also see environments that influence those choices. In addition, social workers understand that the interaction between persons and environments may result in trauma. For some, trauma may result in an inability to take advantage of or even perceive opportunities. But, Flexner talked about a professional activity, and professional spirit is more than this.

Reconciling the Denotation and the Connotation

Could it be that "professional spirit" is the imperative to engage in social work professional activity bounded by the ethical code toward both individual and social impact? For any student interested in adopting the social work professional spirit, it is a call toward critical assessment and intervention at all ecological systems levels, to engage in sustainable change with individuals, families, groups, organizations, and communities. Not as a choice, but as an imperative. It is a consideration of the fullness and breadth of human existence, and a life supporting health and well-being in its perception and opportunity.

CHAPTER 3

LEARNING ACTIVITIES

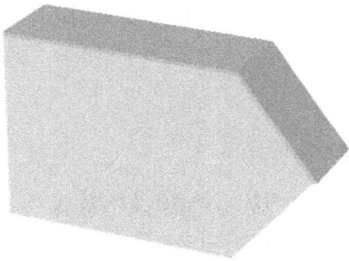

eview a brief history of the initial challenges faced by social workers. Compare and contrast the status of professions commonly held by women historically and day.

WRITING ASSIGNMENT

Compare and contrast the professional attributes of psychology, sociology, and social work.

Chapter 3: Establishing the Social Work Profession

MARY RICHMOND'S TASK

The 1870s - 1900 witnessed the emergence of Charity Organization Societies (COS). While social workers gained title, the first Annual National Conference of Charities and Correction (NCCC) convened in 1874.

It was at one of these conferences in 1915 that Abraham Flexner outlined the requirements for professional legitimacy in 1915. Flexner's address to the NCCC posited that social work had NOT yet achieved professional status.

Mary Richmond had assumed the rather challenging task of defining social work in 1899 with her book, "Friendly Visiting Among the Poor." "Friendly Visiting Among the Poor" is written such that the chapters are a by-environment view of casework. The text seemed to highlight the value of examining multiple environments and perspectives in assessing the client.

Richmond continued her contribution, eventually spanning 30 years, attempting to frame and reframe the profession in the context of emerging science. She had to both provide an educational foundation for the core skills and differentiate the profession from other helping professions.

In 1917, the same year that the National Social Workers Exchange began job placement activities in social work positions, Mary Richmond published "Social Diagnosis." This new text established the guidelines and norms for professional social work practice. "Social Diagnosis" centered on the case management process. It differed from the 1899 text by approaching the case more objectively arguably as a nod to Flexner's "knowledge, not routine" requirement. It should be noted that Richmond also made a presentation to the renamed National Conference of Social Work in 1917. She seemed to rebut Flexner's argument in her speech.

Professional organizations continue to form representing cohesion of social work professionals. Albeit, the differences in practice environments are clear.

1922 Mary Richmond writes "What is social casework?" The tone of this work moves away from the psychoanalytics, which "Social Diagnosis" seemed to be more comfortable with. This new work sought to distinguish social casework through a careful exclusionary definition differentiating social casework from the science of other behavioral practitioners. Mary Richmond defined social case work as "those processes which develop personality through adjustments consciously effected, individual by individual, between men and their social environment."

In 1928, Mary Richmond dies. Over the next 25 years, many other organizations form highlighting the various fields of practice shaping the profession.

By the early 1950's, Social work practice is divided into three foci: casework, group work, and community work. If you read texts from that era, you will invariably encounter discussions about integrating the professional foci, arguing against professional fragmentation. The splintering remains a topic today with discussions of individual practice, also called micro practice; group practice, also called mezzo practice; and community practice, also called macro practice.

MORE OF THE TIMELINE

1918 American Association of Medical Social Workers,

1919 National Association of School Social Workers,

1921 American Association of Social Workers.

1926 American Association of Psychiatric Social Workers formed.

1928 Mary Richmond dies.

1936 Study Group American Association of Group Workers formed.

1946 American Association of Group Workers formed.

1946 Association for the Study of Community Organization formed.

1949 Social Work Research Group formed.

In **1955**, National Association of Social Workers (NASW) formed from all professional organizations in existence.

In **1957**, Ernest Greenwood presents the 5 attributes of a profession credited by some as silencing the objections of Flexner concerning the professional status of social work.

Bibliographic Notes

Many of Mary Richmond's works, such as What is Social Casework? An Introductory Description (1922), are available free of charge from Google Books. View them and contrast her definitions of social work from friendly visiting, to diagnosis, to casework.

David M. Austin provides some important points about the evolution of the National Conference on Charities and Corrections (NCCC) in his 1983 article appearing in Social Service Review. He highlights the fact that the conference was renamed in 1916 as the National Conference of Social Work under the direction of new president Jane Addams (p. 360).

[WRITING EXAMPLE] Professional Attributes of Social Work

A single set of attributes can be derived by combining the work of Flexner (1915) and Greenwood (1957).

The phrasing of each of the attribute lists makes it difficult to come up with a single list. The combination is also frustrated because language, especially professional words, changes and takes on new meanings over time. As if the variance between 1915 and 1957 are not enough, creating a list in the current lexicon adds another 50+ years of variability.

Rephrasing, utilizing more current terms, produces a useful list of social work professional attributes. The attributes are as follows: Theoretical Basis, Identified Approach, Observability, Political Standing, Practical Settings, and a Code of Ethical Conduct. These attributes are useful in describing the social work profession and determining the elements that constitute mastery of the skills of the profession.

-o-

SECTION II: PROFESSIONAL ATTRIBUTES OF THE SOCIAL WORK PROFESSION

CHAPTER 4

LEARNING ACTIVITIES

Review the general and specific values that guide professional social workers. Discuss the pros and cons of self-determination.

WRITING ASSIGNMENT

Discuss how you will integrate your personal and professional values.

Chapter 4: The Social Work Code of Ethics

CORE VALUES OR ETHICAL PARAMETERS

As we begin a review of social work values and ethics, let us agree on three definitions: Principles, Ethics, and Values. Principles are statements of fundamental truth that you accept, which form the basis of all other truths (e.g. values, morals, etc.). Ethics are a behavioral expression of principles. Values refer to the things you prefer. They are the things that you see as ideal.

The core values of social work, as identified in the National Association of Social Workers (NASW) Code of Ethics are service, social justice, dignity and worth of the person, importance of human relationships, integrity, and competence. Explore the reasoning behind these values, the principle truths.

Service may be thought of as reflecting the truth that a holistic contribution to society is both individual and social in nature.

Social justice may be a reasoned response to the fact that majority rule creates minorities whose voices must be heard.

Dignity and worth of the person recognizes that each human has a valuable contribution to make to the collective end product.

The importance of human relationships reflects the truth that realities are collaboratively created.

Integrity may be thought of as reflecting the truth that healthy relationships are based in trust.

Competence recognizes that clear role definition supports collaborative health.

SECTIONS OF THE SOCIAL WORK CODE

The Code of Ethics of the National Association of Social Workers (NASW) does not seek to silence disagreements among social workers seeking to resolve ethical issues. The code does spell out values, principles, and standards to be considered by ethical social workers. The code is presented in six sections.

Section 1 describes the social workers' ethical responsibilities to clients. This section includes the statement on self-determination, which upholds the right of the client to self-determine unless she poses an imminent threat to herself or others.

Section 2 describes the social workers' ethical responsibilities to colleagues. This section, among other responsibilities, instructs social workers to seek to resolve matters when a colleague is perceived to have acted unethically by discussing concerns with the colleague. If the matter cannot be resolved after talking with the colleague, social workers are compelled to report the offense through appropriate channels.

Section 3 describes the social workers' ethical responsibilities in practice settings. The section includes responsibilities in supervision, education, evaluation, administration, staff development, and employment.

Section 4 describes the social workers' ethical responsibilities as professionals. In addition to other responsibilities, this section of the code admonishes professional social workers to engage in private conduct that does not interfere with professional responsibilities. Another important responsibility in this section is the admonishment to seek consultation when personal problems may interfere with professional judgment.

Section 5 describes the social workers' ethical responsibilities to the social work profession. In this section, in addition to responsibilities related to evaluation and research, social workers are instructed to contribute to the knowledge base of the profession and seek to contribute to the literature of the profession.

Section 6 describes the social workers' ethical responsibilities to the broader society. This section sets a standard for social workers to promote the general welfare of society, facilitate informed civic participation, help in public emergencies, and act to ensure equal access, expand choice, encourage respect, prevent and eliminate domination, exploitation, and discrimination.

Bibliographic Notes

The complete Social Work Code of Ethics may be found at *socialworkers.org/pubs/code/* . Read the code of ethics and highlight passages that are unclear to you. Discuss your thoughts with a peer.

[WRITING EXAMPLE] Personal and Professional Value Integration

Personal and professional values must be integrated or the social worker risks dissociation and an unsustainable mental health trajectory. Social workers must abide by the code of ethics whether they are formally representing the profession in a job or if they are conducting personal business. It stands to reason that the social worker cannot professionally uphold a value like dignity and worth of the person, yet contradict that value in his/her personal life.

However, social workers must be able to take off the professional hat in order to lead a normal personal life. A social worker cannot maintain mental health is he/she broods or agonizes over cases and the plight of every client. He/she must release this anxiety through some form of stress coping, supervision, or a combination.

Personal-Professional Value Integration is a state of functioning in which the social worker both maintains congruence between personal and professional values AND manages personal challenges and professional challenges separately. It is misleading to simply state, "Leave work at work and let your home life be home life." It may be more realistic to counsel, "Maintain congruence between your personal and professional values. Separate emotions, diagnoses, and details in your professional practice from the stress, coping, or relationship that is personal." Above all, practice the same ethical values both personally and professionally.

-o-

CHAPTER 5

LEARNING ACTIVITIES

eview the professional authority of the social work profession gained from accredited educational standards. Consider the value of accrediting social ork programs.

WRITING ASSIGNMENT

Discuss how educational degrees and certifications fit into your larger professional goals.

Chapter 5: Social Work Education

CORE CONCEPTS AND ACCREDITATION

Six topic areas form the core of social work education:

- Human Behavior in the Social Environment, often called HBSE for short;

- Social Work Practice, with individuals, families, groups, and communities (IFGOC);

- Social Welfare Policy;

- Social Research;

- Social Work Practicum, also called Field; and

- Social Work Values & Ethics.

Human Behavior in the Social Environment, often called HBSE for short, explores human systems across the life span. Of particular interest is the ways in which social systems, including economic and political environments, support of hinder health and well-being. HBSE provides the foundation for social work theories of assessment, intervention, evaluation, and social worker roles.

Social Work Practice explores social worker roles, contexts, and leadership for intervention with individuals, families, and groups and innovation of organizations and communities. Often, social workers speak of evidence-based practice to communicate proven activities for intervention and innovation. Social work utilizes research, technological advances, and best practices gained through thoughtful reflections on practice.

Social Welfare Policy explores the policies and services that impact social and economic well-being. History is a large aspect of this educational core. Social workers are educated for social action, advocacy, evaluation of service delivery, and policy creation. Advancement of human rights and social and economic justice are of particular interest.

Social Research explores the process for consuming research, creating evidence for interventions and innovations, evaluating practice, and translating research into best practices. "Social workers comprehend quantitative and qualitative research and understand scientific and ethical approaches to building knowledge" (CSWE EPAS, p. 5). Social research is the primary way that social workers implement the Code of Ethics Section 5 requirement to contribute to the professional knowledge base.

Social Work Practicum, also called Field explores, is the signature pedagogy of social work education. This means that social workers teach and learn through the role, function, and practice of the social worker at work. In the lower division classroom, this will translate into reality-based examples, case studies, and role plays. In upper division course work, this will translate into an actual student learning experience called field education. In Field Education, the social work student will complete 400 or more hours of supervised and coordinated professional practice at an actual community-facing agency.

Social Work Values & Ethics explores the social workers identity as a professional including core values, appreciation of diversity and difference, concern for human rights and justice, as well as personal-professional value integration. This content is often infused throughout the social work education curriculum. This means that each course leads students in some reflection on values and ethics. Specific courses in values and ethics may explore the resolution of ethical dilemmas, ethical reasoning, or appreciation of specific differences like culture or religion.

COMPETENCIES & ACCREDITATION

Competence in social work education in the United States is ensured through a process of accreditation. Accreditation is a peer-review process or quality assurance that certifies the credibility and authority of educational services based on a set of competencies.

The accrediting body for social work in the United States is the Council on Social Work Education (CSWE). The CSWE was founded in 1952 and is recognized by the Council for Higher Education Accreditation as the sole accrediting agency for social work education in the United States.

As of the February 2015 Commission on Accreditation meeting, there are

- 504 accredited baccalaureate social work programs,
- 235 accredited master of social work programs,
- 16 baccalaureate social work programs in candidacy, and
- 19 master of social work programs in candidacy (cswe.org).

CSWE produces accreditation standards as the guidelines for structuring and evaluating all social work educational programs. The most recent update of these standards was completed in 2015. The Educational Policy and Accreditation Standards (EPAS) of 2015 provide standards for Program Mission & Goals, Implicit Curriculum, Explicit Curriculum, and Assessment.

Program Mission & Goals requires articulation of the mission, goals, values, and context of the social work educational program. Social work programs are encouraged to respond with specific attention to context—the sense of place, culture, and service opportunities of program location.

Implicit Curriculum incorporates considerations of the learning environment including diversity, student progression & development, faculty qualifications, administrative and governance structure, and resources.

Explicit Curriculum describes requirements related to the curriculum and field placement. It also defines generalist and specialized practice. Field Education is presented as the signature pedagogy of social work. Nine competencies are required to be evidenced and assessed in every accredited social work program across the United States.

The 2015 EPAS included the following 9 competencies:
1. Demonstrate Ethical and Professional Behavior
2. Engage Diversity and Difference in Practice
3. Advance Human Rights and Social, Economic, and Environmental Justice
4. Engage in Practice-Informed Research and Research-Informed Practice
5. Engage in Policy Practice
6. Engage with Individuals, Families, Groups, Organizations, and Communities
7. Assess Individuals, Families, Groups, Organizations, and Communities
8. Intervene with Individuals, Families, Groups, Organizations, and Communities
9. Evaluate Practice with Individuals, Families, Groups, Organizations, and Communities

Assessment requires that programs evaluate all areas of their operations each year. Social work programs are required by the 2015 EPAS to represent competence as holistic including the traditional knowledge, values and skills of the profession, but also the critical thinking, affective reflections, and professional judgments commonly resulting from a liberal arts education. A detailed report called a self-study is due periodically to maintain accreditation of a program. Self-study includes the each of the elements described by the EPAS: program mission and goals, implicit curriculum, explicit curriculum and assessment. The 2015 EPAS is the first in recent history to require multi-dimensional assessment of each student including individual demonstration of competence. Assessment must be used to inform the decision making and innovation in each social work program.

GENERALIST EDUCATION PROGRESSION

Social work education has adopted a generalist model of education identifying levels of education as follows:

- Generalist refers to a breath of knowledge in each of the core content areas. Generalists are to have the knowledge, skills, and attitudes to perform as a professional across the lifespan and across multiple systems.

- Advanced Generalist refers to the ability to supervise others in their professional application of social work knowledge, skills, and attitudes. Advanced Generalist have the ability to instruct and evaluate the practice of professional social work.

- Specialization refers to a depth of knowledge in a specific practice context. Social work specializations exist in child welfare, gerontology, community organization, and others.

At the undergraduate level, all programs are generalist. At the master degree level, programs choose to develop either advanced generalist or specializations. Generally, master degree programs describe program focus with phrases like clinical practice or administrative. Within these broad system level descriptions, the program may have additional specializations.

Emphases are another way to differentiate between Master level degree program. Emphases may be offered in social administration, palliative care, marriage & family, community research, or policy.

SOCIAL WORK EDUCATION PROGRESSION

It may be useful to think of social work education as a progression toward increasing autonomy in practice. For social workers, autonomy is most often represented in the ability to bill insurance companies.

The progression of social work education can be visualized as a pyramid: Level 1 Pre-Professional, Level 2 Generalist, Level 3 Advanced Generalist, Level 4 Evaluation, and Level 5 Empirical Research.

Level 1 Pre-Professional includes Liberal Arts and Basic Skills.

Students are typically introduced to Social Work Professional Ethics, Civic Engagement & Service Learning, and Cultural Competence. They may be taught Interviewing with a model such as the Generalist Intervention Model (GIM). Many social work education programs also offer Social Welfare History & Services content in Level 1.

Many programs, though designating students as majors, do not consider them social work majors until the students complete a formal acceptance into the BSW program. This application and review process typically occurs at the conclusion of Level 1 Pre-Professional.

Level 2 Generalist

Level 2 seeks to integrate Liberal arts content into theories of Human Behavior, Policy, Research and Social Work Values & Ethics. Students are taught specific Social Work Practice Methods with the goal of informing Case Management and Community Analysis. Students complete a Social Work Field Practicum for a minimum of 400 hours.

For undergraduate students, completion of Level 2 qualifies them for graduation with a BSW degree. For graduate students, Level 2 is the first year of the MSW program. This relationship between the final two years of the Bachelor of social work degree and the first year of the Master of social work degree means that BSW graduates who qualify may complete the MSW degree in one additional year.

Level 3 Advanced Generalist

Level 3 provides the student with perspectives on Social Justice, Advocacy and Organizing, and Practice Evaluation. Social Work Methods and Ethics in Level 3 focus on developing skills in Direct Client Change (intervention) and Systems Change (policy). Students complete a Social Work Field Practicum for a minimum of 600 hours.

At the conclusion of Level 3, students graduate with the Master of Social Work (MSW) degree. But, professional development does not end there.

Level 4 Evaluation

Level 4 is a conceptualization of the first stage of post-MSW practice. This Level focuses on informing research questions through reflective practice and consumption of research and evidence-based practice. Typically, MSWs are able to explore and create Grounded Theory through the Evaluation of Practice Models (Practice Evaluation).

Level 5 Empirical Research is a conceptualization of the subsequent stage of post-MSW practice. This level focuses on evaluating research questions in order to contribute to the knowledge base of social work. Social work researchers create evidence-based practice through Empirical Analysis Informing new Practice Models.

[See the Table: Generalist Education Progression]

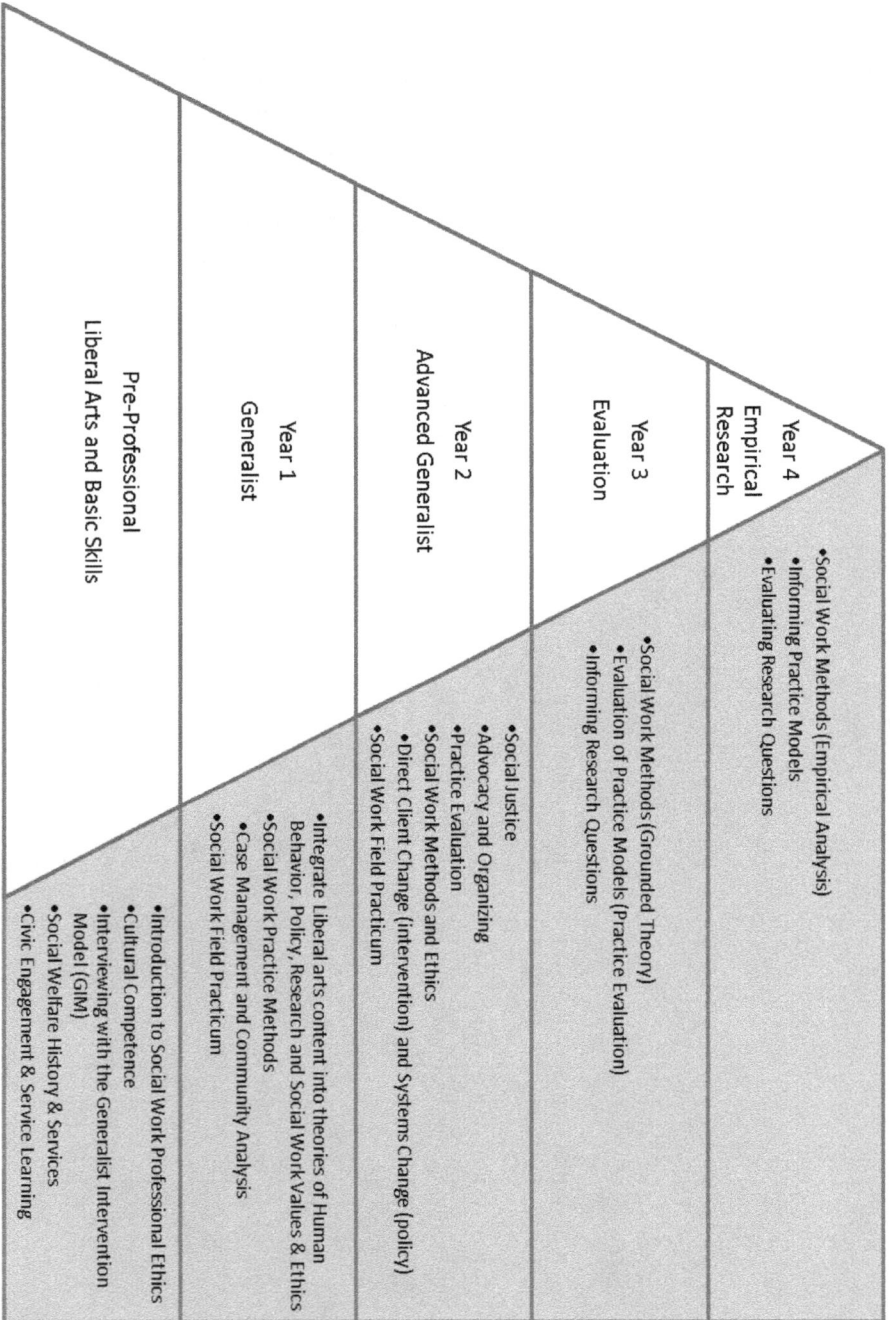

Year 4
Empirical Research
- Social Work Methods (Empirical Analysis)
- Informing Practice Models
- Evaluating Research Questions

Year 3
Evaluation
- Social Work Methods (Grounded Theory)
- Evaluation of Practice Models (Practice Evaluation)
- Informing Research Questions

Year 2
Advanced Generalist
- Social Justice
- Advocacy and Organizing
- Practice Evaluation
- Social Work Methods and Ethics
- Direct Client Change (intervention) and Systems Change (policy)
- Social Work Field Practicum

Year 1
Generalist
- Integrate Liberal arts content into theories of Human Behavior, Policy, Research and Social Work Values & Ethics
- Social Work Practice Methods
- Case Management and Community Analysis
- Social Work Field Practicum

Pre-Professional
Liberal Arts and Basic Skills
- Introduction to Social Work Professional Ethics
- Cultural Competence
- Interviewing with the Generalist Intervention Model (GIM)
- Social Welfare History & Services
- Civic Engagement & Service Learning

Bibliographic Notes

The Council on Social Work Education (CSWE) Educational Policy and Accreditation Standards (EPAS) document is available at *http://www.cswe.org/File.aspx?id=79793.* All accredited social work degree programs must adhere to this policy document. It should be noted that the CSWE hosts an Annual Program Meeting, a conference, which invites students to attend, volunteer, and interact with educators primarily from around the United States but including representatives from outside the US.

[WRITING EXAMPLE] Defending Competency-Based Education

Competency-based education (CBE) is a great innovation in educational practice. When knowledge, skills, and values are ordered in modules and evaluated as competencies, students can work toward mastery of content. Teachers can evaluate mastery without getting lost in the aggregate score of the examination or course.

Yet, CBE does have some critics. Some say that, implemented by novices, CBE may support teaching to the test. Teachers may abandon the progression and structure of the curriculum in order to get students through the coursework. Students who achieve 80% proficiency suffer from the 20% they did not master that is critical to the next module.

Even with the critics, CBE remains an important innovation in education. It is true that teachers require the proper training and experience with CBE methods. It is also true that students who complete modular learning and achieve mastery can better partner with teachers to reflect on their learning. This metacognition will serve the student beyond the current course toward an awareness of his/her own learning.

-o-

CHAPTER 6

LEARNING ACTIVITIES

Review the community sanction of the social work profession both informal and formal. Contrast the respect level of four ofessions including social work.

WRITING ASSIGNMENT

Describe the impact that you wish to make on your community.

Chapter 6: Definition of a Social Worker, Title Protection, and Licensure

DEFINITION

The International Federation of Social Workers adopted a definition of social work in 2000. The IFSW definition reads:

> "The social work profession promotes social change, problem solving in human relationships and the empowerment and liberation of people to enhance well-being. Utilising theories of human behaviour and social systems, social work intervenes at the points where people interact with their environments. Principles of human rights and social justice are fundamental to social work" (ifsw.org).

The IFSW provides a caveat on their website explaining that no one definition of social work is exhaustive. Indeed, many social workers would say that the definition of a social worker is broad.

Many would point to definitions provided by organizations like the National Association of Social Workers or the aforementioned IFSW. Definitions will invariably mention aspects of the core values of social work: service, social justice, dignity and worth of the person, the importance of human relationships, integrity, and competence.

Legal definitions of a social worker center on two actions taken by many states: Title Protection and Licensure. These two actions, though not producing universal definitions of a social worker, do specify who can represent themselves as a professional social worker.

HELPING PROFESSIONS AND TITLES

Social work is one of a number of helping professions. The other helping professions are nursing, pharmacy, medicine, psychological counseling, and education. The social work code of ethics forbids social workers from misrepresenting themselves and their training. Many states have enacted laws that prohibit others from misrepresenting themselves as social workers.

This type of state law is often called **Title Protection**. Title Protection most often limits the moniker of social worker to those who have graduated from a college or university accredited by the Council on Social Work Education. Title protection has been an important issue in many states for social workers and other helping professionals including, nurses and pharmacists most notably.

LICENSURE

States and provinces administer licensing boards in order to register individuals as helping professionals. Many state social work licensing boards provide licenses at all levels of education BSW, MSW and PhD.

Most state boards distinguish between clinical social workers and social workers in other areas of practice. A clinical license is only available for professionals who possess a Master degree in social work and two years of supervision after receiving the Master degree.

In most states, applicants for a license must provide proof of the appropriate education and take a test upon completion of the degree. Tests are produced by the Association of Social Work Boards (ASWB) and are administered at testing centers located throughout the country. Yet, state licensure boards set the policies for levels of licensure, allowable activities, and experience requirements.

BSW graduates are able to receive licenses in many states. Acronyms vary from state to state, and may be listed as LBSW, RSW, and LSW among others. Allowable activities at this level of licensure usually relate to what is termed generalist practice. Generalist practice includes work in information and referral for individuals, families, groups, organizations, and communities.

MSW graduates may be listed as LMSW, LGSW, or LISW among others. Allowable activities at this level include advanced generalist practice. Advanced generalist practice may include supervised utilization of diagnostic manuals for social workers preparing for clinical licensure, and community advocacy, administration, or organizing for non-clinical social workers.

Graduates with more than two years of supervised experience as an advanced generalist are eligible for clinical licensure. Many states list clinical social workers with an LCSW credential. States like Tennessee also have a license designation for non-clinical social workers with more than two years of experience. The Tennessee social work board lists non-clinical, advanced generalist social workers with experience as LAPSW, licensed advanced practice social workers.

LCSW social workers are able to diagnose clients utilizing the Diagnostic and Statistical Manual (DSM). These social workers also join the short list of professionals who are able to bill insurance companies in the state for services rendered.

Rules, listings, and regulations vary. Specific questions can be answered by the social work board of your state or province.

Bibliographic Notes

The *ASWB.org* website lists contact information for state and provincial governments. Review the title protection and/or licensure law covering social work in your state. Review testing rules for your state at the Association of Social Work Boards website.

[WRITING EXAMPLE] Social Work as a Health Care Profession

It should be news to no one that social work is a health care profession. Social workers are concerned with the biology, psychology, social, and spiritual aspects of clients. Medical fields since Engel in 1977 have recognized the same. The mental health is inextricable from the physical health. That means that social workers are an important part of any health care discussion.

Few would argue with the characterization of social work as a helping profession, but some may question whether it is a health care profession. The social work focus on biology is often simply to rule out medical causes for behavioral manifestations. It would stand to reason that more psychopharmacology, anatomy & physiology, and neurobiology would better inform social workers who wanted to be conversant in health care discussions. A medical terminology course is at least warranted.

Both can be true. Social workers could benefit from an expansion of human behavior in the social environment content that references advances in mind-body connection and the effects of medications. What critics may not know is that social work in health care offers the added opportunity to influence behavior change. This can work to the advantage of prevention efforts, rehabilitation, and addictions recovery—three important focal points for modern medical practice.

-o-

CHAPTER 7

LEARNING ACTIVITIES

List the major social work professional organizations. List the pros and cons of maintaining separate organizations rather an one central organization.

WRITING ASSIGNMENT

List ways that specific organizations can help you achieve your goals.

Chapter 7: Social Work Professional Organizations

Following is a listing of many social work professional organizations that have a national presence. Notice features and information typically available from each.

NASW stands for the National Association of Social Workers. Founded in 1955, the organization is the lead advocacy group for the social work profession. If you were looking for information on the history of the profession or the code of ethics, this would be the organization to contact first. The NASW website (naswdc.org) boasts a consumer information portal and a feature detailing the lives of many social work pioneers throughout history.

ASWB stands for the Association of Social Work Boards. In addition to its work in developing and maintaining licensing examinations for the US and some Canadian provinces, ASWB periodically conducts an analysis of the practice of social work to aid in updating its examinations.

The website (aswb.org) lists exam sites, content outlines, a registry, and all things licensure related. If you are looking for information on the licensing regulations for a specific state, ASWB can link you to the information quickly.

CSWE stands for the Council on Social Work Education. Founded in 1952, CSWE is the sole accrediting body for social work education in the United States. You can find information on its accredited social work programs and programs seeking accreditation on the CSWE website (cswe.org). Another important find on the CSWE website is the Educational Policy and Accreditation Standards (EPAS). This document outlines the regulations for social work education.

BPD stands for Baccalaureate Program Directors. The official title of the organization is the Association of Baccalaureate Program Directors. BPD produces a journal primarily focused on undergraduate issues and soliciting both faculty and student manuscripts in social work. The listerv maintained by the association may be just as popular as the website (bpdonline.org).

ACOSA stands for the Association for Community Organization & Social Administration. The association reminds everyone that, in addition to work with individuals and families, social workers practice with groups and communities. View web information at acosa.org.

SSWR stands for the Society for Social Work and Research. Chartered in 1993, the society seeks to involve all social workers in research. Like other associations, SSWR offers a journal and an annual conference. More information is available at sswr.org.

NSWM stands for the Network for Social Work Management. The association seeks to equip and support social workers working at all levels of management in human services organizations.

NSWM has compiled competencies and administers the Certified Social Work Manager (CSWM) credential. The journal produced by NSWM is entitled Administration in Social Work. More information is online at socialworkmanager.org.

Bibliographic Notes

National Association of Social Workers
NASWDC.org

Association of Social Work Boards
ASWB.org

Council on Social Work Education
CSWE.org

Association of Baccalaureate Program Directors
BPDonline.org

Association for Community Organization and Social Administration
ACOSA.org

Society for Social Work and Research
SSWR.org

Network for Social Work Management
socialworkmanager.org

[WRITING EXAMPLE] The Case for a Single Social Work Organization

It was 1955 when the social work organizations in existence unified to create what we know today as the National Association of Social Workers. It is time for the same spirit of unification to rapture the profession. The synergies, resource sharing, expertise, and membership pooling could be game changing.

But, a single, combined organization may not fully capture the diversity of the organizations that are now operating. The various concerns, approaches, sensitivities to politics, research, levels of practice and more could be muted with a move to one single organization. It would be a grand feat to create an organization that large that would provide a sense of individual attention to each of its members.

A possible compromise may be achieved by combining something other than the organizational operations. Let us launch a study of the political, economic, social, and technological interests of each of the current social work organizations. With this report, it may be possible to collaborate on redundant activities and streamline the issues most dear to each organization. This could result in more efficient resource usage, greater advantage to diversity, and a more unified voice even if the organizational operations are not unified under one unit.

-o-

SECTION III: THE SCIENCE OF THE SOCIAL WORK PROFESSION

CHAPTER 8

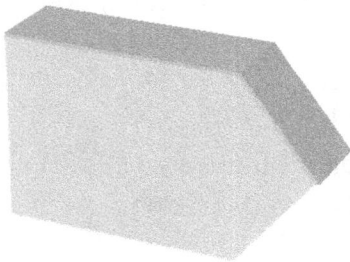

LEARNING ACTIVITIES

Review the general and specific knowledge that guide professional social workers. Consider the combined value of sessment and intervention.

WRITING ASSIGNMENT

Describe how you will utilize HBSE theory to understand a problem. List some common barriers to making sustainable choices.

Chapter 8: Systematic Body of Theory: HBSE

Good/Bad or Sustainable/Unsustainable?

Rather than seeing choices as good or bad, the job of the social worker is to intervene for more sustainable choice behavior toward psychosocial wellbeing. Psychosocial wellbeing describes a healthy mental state as well as health in the relationships that influence change. The psychological portion of psychosocial wellbeing includes intelligence, access, and awareness of options. The sociological portion of psychosocial wellbeing includes relationships with individuals as well as interactions with environmental influences such as institutions.

Social workers recognize that choice is motivated at a behavioral level by positively reinforcement or negatively reinforcement. Positively reinforcing choice is a choice you will continue to make because it provides rewards. Negatively reinforcing choice is a choice that you will continue to make because it prevents or removes something that you do not like.

Individuals make unsustainable choices. But, the key to intervening toward behavior change is to figure out why the choice continues to be made, even though it appears to be unsustainable. The answer may involve positive reinforcement or negative reinforcement.

Positive Reinforcement example:

You self-medicate alcohol because you reason that alcohol use allows you to forget your problems rather than deal with them directly.

Negative Reinforcement example:

You never share your poetry and reason that you never have to risk an unfavorable review.

What social workers notice in these examples is that the determination of the "WHY" requires identification of the goals the client holds as important. The client does not act within a vacuum. The relationships and institutions impact behavior choice. The environment also has some impact on choice. Social work has a vocabulary and organization for articulating these.

The Science of Social Work

Social work is a science. It is more than just doing good. It is more than "helping people." Yet, most students come to the profession with some version of a desire to "help people and do good." In their education, they learn to become a professional trained to map and change behavior through behavioral economics, institutional change processes, and environmental practice.

Like scientists, professional social workers dismiss the idea of certainty and operate on a reasoned approach to observing, predicting, and influencing social outcomes. The central body of theory undergirding this science is termed human behavior in the social environment. HBSE, pronounced *hibsee* for short, provides a vocabulary and explores a number of concepts that influence behavior choice. The Human Behavior concepts include individual choice, trauma, and capacity/confidence. The social environment concepts include social influences, structural/institutional pressures, and historical pressures.

HBSE includes a number of what we may call Large Frame Concepts to which it brings a unique perspective. Large Frame Concepts can be organized into four categories: Influencing Behavior, Interaction Ethics, Assessment Perspectives, and Intervention Methods.

Influencing Behavior

Synergy in Human Systems suggests that humans have the ability to change as a result of interactions. It is important, though, that professional social work consider ethical interactions toward change. Equifinality, boundaries, and structure of transaction are three concepts to promote ethical interaction toward change.

Systemic Change, in social work, is focused on affecting systems and the relationships among them. Systems can experience internal integration, in which change occurs motivated by the system itself. Systems can also experience external adaptation, in which change occurs motivated by other systems or the environment of the systems. Social work draws on a number of sources for exploring and articulating change at micro, mezzo, and macro systems levels.

Role is an important concept in social work. Social workers recognize that the individual may assume a variety of roles throughout the day that impact her choices. Roles also occur simultaneously. At a dinner party, a 24 year old female could simultaneously have the role of mother, co-worker, employee, wife, and sister. Choices of what to eat, wear, say, and other choices are influenced by these roles.

Interrelatedness is a concept that reminds social workers that relationships are reciprocal. Because of interrelatedness, social workers understand that behavior is not only an action but it can also be reaction to others or the environment.

Interaction Ethics

Equifinality suggests that multiple activities can produce the same results. Social workers seek solutions that are best based on a thorough assessment, and weigh factors that suggest one choice as better than others. The factors include fit and relevance to the client as primary.

Boundaries identify what is out of bounds in the change relationship. The level of interaction in professional practice is set to the level of the client understanding so that interactions do not threaten the ability of the individual to reasonably self-determine.

Structure of Transaction is an approach to interaction contracting in which both parties agree upon what is to be offered as payment. Humans want to be reciprocal. Structure of transaction identifies proper ways to celebrate successes, integrate learning, and complete the transaction.

Assessment Perspectives

Social work theory begins with a perspective on systems. The ecological systems perspective advanced by Bronfenbrenner provides a framework for exploring the connections and the relationships among systems. The **ecological systems perspective** has five descriptors: micro, meso, exo, macro, and chronosystem. Ecomaps are used to visually represent the relationships among systems. Micro and meso systems are nested within the macro system. Exo systems also exist within the macro system but are not nested. The chronosystem describes the interactions of systems over time.

Person-In-Environment refers to a perspective in social work assessment. It holds that assessment of the total person includes an awareness of the person in her environment. Every person seeks balance AND this balance is often a reaction to external events and pressures.

The **Biopsychosocial perspective** originated with Engel (1977), a medical doctor, who questioned why patients receiving the same care responded with different outcomes. He sought to explain the variation in outcomes promoting a holistic approach to health care. Many social work professionals add an additional component, "spirituality" to the biopsychosocial assessment.

Social workers employ the biopsychosocial-spiritual perspective to holistically assess clients and explain the influences on choice. The perspective can be used to formulate questions. The answers to these questions form the basis of a biopsychosocial assessment.

- Biology asks: Is the choice age appropriate and not the result of disease?

- Psychology asks: Is the choice an informed choice characterized by an awareness of all options?

- Sociology asks: What expectations, pressures, or influences are present? Are external expectations balanced by internal motivations and ownership of the choice?

- Spirituality asks: Are there elements that are not constrained by what can be perceived and measured?

Intervention Models

HBSE provides a framework for social workers to influence behavior through Assessment & Intervention. Assessment is a systematic process. It provides information to the social worker about how the client understands choices and their consequences.

Intervention involves explaining the process that has been assessed. The client is assisted to understand what may have led to the current state. The social worker then shares an intervention plan that can retrain the habit behaviors and provide new choices.

The history of social work suggests variations in approaches to assessment and intervention in different contexts such as casework, group work, and community organizing. Generalist approaches can be useful to work across contexts while maintaining professional depth to intervene in significant ways.

The Generalist Intervention Model (GIM) and the Stages of Change Process are two approaches to assessment and intervention that, with little modification, can be applied to casework, group work, and community organizing.

The **Generalist Intervention Model (GIM)** was popularized by Kirst-Ashman and Hull (2006). It has seven steps: engagement, assessment, planning, implementation, evaluation, termination, and follow-up. Utilizing work from Cournoyer (2011), Wright (2012) presented GIM+ adding Preparation as a first step in the model.

GIM+ also delineates attitudes and behaviors specific to each of the model's steps.

The **Stages of Change Process** is also referred to as the Transtheoretical Model (TTM). It was originally developed in addictions treatment but has been applied in community work as well. It has six steps: Pre-contemplation, Contemplation, Preparation, Action, Maintenance, and Positive Exit or Relapse. Each step offers a chance to move toward goal achievement building on the accomplishments of the prior step. In the final stage, Positive Exit or Relapse, the client sustains a productive lifestyle or returns to unsustainable choice behavior.

Summary

Social work is a science working to support sustainable choice behavior through individual, institutional, and environmental change practice. Human Behavior in the Social Environment (HBSE) organizes large frame concepts to inform this change imperative. This knowledge allows social workers to influence behavior, ethically interact, assess, and intervene with clients across multiple systems.

[WRITING EXAMPLE] **Why Social Workers Don't Do Therapy**

Social workers are not therapists. It is a mistake to assume that even clinical social workers, with two years of experience, are therapists. First, use of the term "therapist" or "therapy" may not fit the competence and treatment perspective of the social worker. Second, professional social work maintains an equal value on the therapeutic and non-therapy activities of the profession.

The confusion related to the term "therapy" may be founded in an incomplete definition of therapy. Therapy, by definition, refers to a medically-based intervention including an identified diagnosis, treatment protocol, and prognosis. Specialized training must support therapy including neurology, psychopharmacology, and social disorders to name a few. It would also be important for a therapist to maintain awareness of new advances in social neurology, biology, and diagnosis guidelines.

The non-therapy assessment and intervention that social workers deliver is valuable as well. Delivering non-therapy assessment and intervention requires the same level commitment to competence and evidence-based research review. Social workers do assess multiple factors including biology, psychology, sociology, and spirituality. They do intervene in change processes that are cognitive, behavioral, and even sense-making. Professional social work interventions boast impact for the individual and the social environment.

Master level, clinical social workers are trained in the use of the diagnostic statistical manual (DSM)—a tool produced by the American Psychological Association and used for diagnosis of clients. Social workers are also trained to develop treatment plans that, as evidence-based protocols. Social research, especially operational research techniques, can be applied to yield predictive models for client outcomes—a prognosis.

Social workers who pursue additional training in the integration of biochemical information in treatment, use of the DSM, evidence-based protocols, and operational research techniques can portend to provide therapy. They are not licensed to dispense all the medical tools in treatment (such as medications), but Master level social workers, by definition and with additional knowledge, can be termed "therapist."

-o-

CHAPTER 9

LEARNING ACTIVITIES

Review the general and specific skills that guide professional social workers. Consider the value of assisting in the ping process.

WRITING ASSIGNMENT

Detail how you will identify and support the strengths of the client.

Chapter 9: Use of Strengths Perspective and a Solution-Focus

Strengths Perspective

The **Strengths Perspective** is an important view of assessment and intervention for social workers. Rather than focusing on deficits and unhealthy patterns, the strengths perspective focuses on the competence, capacity, and resources of the client. In practice, this means identifying coping abilities that the client already possesses. Beyond coping, strengths perspective means adaptation to a new sustainable choice pattern in line with the client's goals.

The strengths perspective adds at least six important constructs to our discussion of the science of social work. These include plasticity, client primacy, self-determination, resource optimization, empowerment, collaboration, and interactive effects (Saleebey, 2006).

Plasticity has been further clarified by Santrock (2012) in the theory of life-span development. Plasticity is the idea that people change. This is important for the social worker because change is the purpose of the client-worker interaction.

Client primacy means that the client and his/her wishes and goals are the first consideration of the client-worker interaction. The job of the worker is to help the client to reach his/her goals even when there is disagreement on the goals. Social workers support client primacy while influencing sustainable choice behaviors by helping the client to structure goals and behaviors that are congruent. Social workers also increase the sustainable choice options available to the client at the point of decision making.

Self-Determination includes client primacy and adds the ownership of choice. Social workers ensure that clients have the information, support, alternatives, and outcome predictions to make informed choices. The final choice is the client's to make.

Resource optimization makes the wealth of resources available to the client. Often, clients in crisis are not aware of the opportunities and supports that are available in the community. Social workers perform a needed service when they connect clients to community providers and support systems. Emphasis is placed on connecting AND guiding healthy utilization.

Empowerment recognizes that though options are presented to the client, he or she may not have the capacity to take advantage of the opportunity or support. Social workers assess the barriers to service utilization and assist clients to overcome those barriers.

Collaboration refers to the way that social workers engage in their work. Social workers often make connections, refer clients, and seek client overall well-being through collaborative relationships developed as a result of work-day, professional, and political interactions within the community. Agency employment among social workers is less about agency competition and more focused on improving service to the client.

Interactive effects understands that the challenges in system navigation are not the fault of the clients, institutions, or organizations. The challenges are due to the interactions between the parties. Social workers work in all their roles to produce the result of successful system navigation that values service, social justice, dignity and worth of the person, the importance of human relationships, integrity, and competence.

Solution-Focused Brief Therapy (SFBT)

Solution-focused Brief Therapy (SFBT) implements the strengths perspective in a unique way through a specific process of questioning. SFBT questions seek to highlight the strengths and solutions that exist within the client's awareness, the client's capacity for change, and the resources perceived by the client.

Miller and Berg (1995) originally advanced eight SFBT Principles. As a set of concepts specific to social workers, the original eight are expanded as follows:

Individualization. No single approach works for everyone. Social workers must use assessment skills to learn about each client separately within the context of professional knowledge, experience, and modalities.

Option Rich. There are many possible solutions. Social workers must both inform the client of the existence of many possible solutions, and work to make each solution attainable by the client.

Disassociation. The solution and the problem are not necessarily related. Social workers are not to solve the problem as much as they are to indicate a solution that returns desired functioning to the client. Focus on the problem or a clear understanding of the problem are not required for a suitable solution.

Modesty. The simplest and least invasive approach is frequently the best medicine. Social workers work primarily to ensure coping with as little disturbance as possible in the client's routine. Especially in crisis situation, return to a routine is the goal even if it is a new normal.

Adaptability. People can and do get better quickly. Similar to plasticity in the strengths perspective, social workers utilizing SFBT work with the expectation of positive progress by the client. Coping for the immediate term enables adaptation for the long term.

Mutability. Change is happening all the time. A supportive concept for adaptability, mutability adds that all systems are in a constant state of change. Social workers help clients establish routines and models to decipher the systems so that the client can best navigate them.

Strengths. Focus on strengths and resources rather than weaknesses and deficits. This principle is the namesake of the strengths perspective. Social workers utilizing SFBT are vigilant to identify competence, capacity, and resources that are readily available to the client.

Future Orientation. Focus on the future rather than the past. With adaptability and mutability on board, new experiences are possible. Social workers utilize a future orientation to assist clients to create new definitions, new abilities, and new networks for support.

As a practical intervention, SFBT questioning has at least three techniques:

- Miracle Questions,
- Scaling Questions, and
- Exceptions Finding.

With each of the techniques, the first task is to establish a new perspective for the client. The second task is to have the client identify behaviors that would be observed if that new perspective was the current reality.

Miracle Questions

The miracle question attempts to provide the client with a view of the world without the crisis. Magical thinking is another name for the technique and suggests ways to begin the question.

An example of a miracle question:

"If you had a magic wand and could resolve the situation, how would your choices be different?"

Another miracle question example:

"If you woke tomorrow and the problem was gone, what would you be doing?"

Scaling Questions

Scaling questions gauge client perceptions and communicate those perceptions through a number-based relational response. The number allows both client and worker to have a common scale for evaluating perceptions.

Scaling questions have two parts. For example,

> "On a scale from 1 to 10, 10 being mad enough to fight, what would you rate your anger?"

The client may respond with a rating of 7. The social worker would then ask,

> "What would you be doing differently to move that from a 7 to a 5?"

Exceptions Finding

Exceptions finding is a technique for identifying a time that the client was not in crisis. This technique is especially useful for identifying solutions when the client feels as if she has lost capacity or the means to cope or adapt.

Finding exceptions may be asked as a one-step question. For example,

> "Can you think of a time when this was not a problem for you?"

Or, finding exceptions can be asked as a two-part question. For example,

> "What do you see yourself doing 5 years from now?"

After the client answers, the social worker may ask,

> "What would you need to be doing now in order to achieve that 5 year goal?"

Handling Setbacks, Relapses, and Retreats

A great rule to live by was written by Walter and Peller in 1992. They suggest that it SFBT:

There is no failure, only feedback.

And when these setbacks, relapses, or retreats inevitably occur, Miller and Berg (1995) suggest to SFBT practitioners:

If it doesn't work, do something different.

In those two statements you find the best of strengths perspective and SFBT. The client and his/her well-being is a work in progress. It will have challenges and retreats. Social workers work to build client's competence, capacity, and resources to offer the best chance at coping and opportunity for adaptation. The work of a social worker is not to fix. It is to be present, make space for coping, and expand options.

Bibliographic Notes

NASW put together a set of standards for case management in 1992. You can find the standards on the NASW website at: *socialworkers.org/practice/standards/sw_case_mgmt.asp*

Walter, J. L. and Peller, J. E. (1992). Becoming solution-focused in brief therapy. New York, NY: Brunner/Mazel Inc.

de Shazer, S. & Berg, I. K. (1992). Doing therapy: A post-structural re-vision. The Journal of Marital and Family Therapy, 18. 71-82.

de Shazer, S. (1985). Keys to solution in brief therapy. New York: W. W. Norton & Company.

Miller, S. D. & Berg, I. K. (1995). The miracle method: A radically new approach to problem drinking. New York: W. W. Norton & Company.

[WRITING EXAMPLE] **Beyond Coping to Adaptation**

The goal of social workers must be adaptation beyond simple coping. Otherwise, clients will have diminished ability to become self-sufficient. Coping is the ability to react sustainably to an immediate stress or crisis. Adaptation is evidence of a plan to manage resources and stress sustainably so that acute crisis is less likely.

Yet, coping is important alone. Coping means that the client is able to tolerate the stressor, maintain a high level of daily functioning, and move forward with goals he/she sets. Insistence on adaptation could force movement before the client feels comfortable. This could set the client up for failure and a relapse into former unsustainable choices.

Adaptation is a solid goal, but it cannot be forced upon the client. Each social worker must be diligent in assessment and monitoring of client progress, overall health, and coping to know whether to plan adaptation interventions. Successful coping can lead to adaptation and self-sufficiency, but the coping must first be assured.

-o-

CHAPTER 10

LEARNING ACTIVITIES

List the components of empowerment and resilience. Reflect on the effect of adverse childhood experiences on human velopment.

WRITING ASSIGNMENT

Detail how you would ensure that actions are promoting empowerment.

Chapter 10: For Empowerment and Resilience

ACE THEORY

Adverse Childhood Experiences (ACE) is a theory of disease that eliminates the line between mental and physical health. ACE research suggests that adverse childhood experiences lead to disrupted neurodevelopment, leading to social, emotional, and cognitive impairment. This impairment leads to the adoption of health-risk behaviors. These lead to disease, disability, and social problems and, ultimately, early death.

The ACE process may be represented in the following way. Trauma diminishes the choice set available to the individual. The individual chooses from a diminished choice set and creates a personal narrative justifying the choice she made. This choice with its attending narrative results in the presenting health behavior.

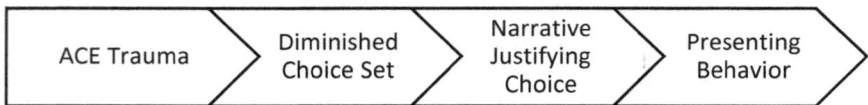

| ACE Trauma | Diminished Choice Set | Narrative Justifying Choice | Presenting Behavior |

Risk factors assessed in ACE surveys include verbal abuse, emotional fearfulness, physical abuse, sexual abuse, family dysfunction, neglect, loss of biological parent, substance abuse in the home, mental illness in an immediate family member, and incarceration of a parent or guardian. Upon completion of the ACE survey, clients are asked, "Tell me how this has affected you later in life?"

RESILIENCE

Identifying trauma and choices is not enough. Social workers help the individual to recognize the power she has to rewrite her personal narrative, increase her choices, and thereby live beyond trauma. The social worker will assess for resilience within the individual. The social worker will intervene with empowerment.

Resilience is defined as the ability to overcome trauma and return to a level of positive functioning. Roberta Greene has researched resilience in children and adults. Resilient individuals have certain attributes, protective features, and psychological characteristics according to Greene. Individuals with higher socioeconomic status tend to be resilient. Other attributes include the absence of organic deficits, possession of an easy temperament, younger age at the time of trauma, and an absence of early separations and losses.

Protective features of resilient children include:

- Competent parenting,
- Good (warm) relationship with at least one primary caregiver,
- Availability (in adulthood) of social support from spouse, family, or other figures,
- Better network of informal relationships, and
- Better formal social support through better education and religious affiliation.

Psychological characteristics of resilient children include:

- high IQ and problem-solving ability,
- superior coping styles,
- task-related self-efficacy,
- autonomy or internal locus of control,

- higher sense of self-worth,

- interpersonal awareness and empathy,

- willingness and capacity to plan, and

- a sense of humor.

EMPOWERMENT

Social workers debate the assertion that any person can be empowered from an external source. But, all social workers agree that empowerment is a necessary condition for overcoming trauma. Empowerment has four dimensions: Experience, Resources, Decision Points, and Structural Controls.

Experience is the feeling of being empowered. It is the expectation that access and opportunity will yield success. The concept of experience is the hinge upon which each of the other dimensions pivot. Empowerment is not only a virtue of helping professions, it can also be thought of as a useful tool in behavior change. Clients who have the expectation of success are more likely to achieve success.

Resources refer to currency for trade and evidence of wealth including information, people, money, and time. An empowered person will feel that she has information that results in an understanding of each available choice and relationships that provide support and diverse voices. Empowerment also means that the individual has the financial capability to make any choice, and choices are not saddled with undue time pressures or anxiety about the timing.

Decision Points are the moments of decision that impact relationships, the environment, and desired outcomes. Choices can be either mandated or reached through shared decision making. Empowerment also means an awareness of the decision points. An empowered person has the autonomy to make decisions at these points even if the choices are contrary to governing authority or social influence.

Structural Controls the set of abilities that enable an individual to apply resources to create and market a product. Structural controls are the means of production. The empowered individual believes that she can impact culture and control her destiny through the choices she makes.

An empowered individual has internal integration, external adaptation, and access to markets. Internal integration is the ability to self-motivate in a planned activity toward an expected outcome. External adaptation is the ability to respond reactively to the environment. Access to markets is the ability to connect a product to the expressed needs present in the environment and benefit from the transaction.

Bibliographic Notes

The CDC is continuing to explore the relationship between adverse childhood experiences, health care use, and causes of death. (http://www.cdc.gov/nccdphp/ACE/, Felitti, et.al. *American Journal of Preventive Medicine*, 1998, Vol. 14, 245-258).

Roberta Greene has produced a great deal of information on resilience across multiple systems and with many different populations. Using information presented in this chapter, consider your level of resilience.

Hardy & Leiba o'Sullivan presented a set of components they called the "dimensions of empowerment" in 1998. Their list included experience, resources, process, and meaning. Informed by agent-based models and Bandura's social agency discussions, meaning is more consistently described as structural controls. Process is more consistently described as decision points.

The concept of experience as presented here is a core tenet in Bandura's development of the concept of self-efficacy. Read Bandura's work and explore the concepts of self-efficacy and social agency.

Bandura, A. (2001). Social cognitive theory: An agentic perspective. Annual Review of Psychology, 52. 1-26. Available Online: *des.emory.edu/mfp/Bandura2001ARPr.pdf*

Bandura, A. (1997). Self-Efficacy: The exercise of control. New York: Macmillan. ISBN: 9780716728504

Hardy, C. and Leiba-O'Sullivan, S. (1998). The power behind empowerment: Implications for research and practice. Human Relations, 51. 451-483.

[WRITING EXAMPLE] The Importance of Decision Points

The concept of decision points is perhaps the most important dimension of empowerment. The choices a client makes are directly correlated with his/her outcomes. Increasing awareness of this fact will go a long way toward enhancing social agency in the client.

Experience is an important dimension as well. If a client does not feel empowered, he/she will not recognize and initiate choices that support success. Experience provides a foundation for self-efficacy. The client must believe that taking action will result in successes.

Experience and decision points work hand in hand. Experience provides the expectation supporting motivation. Decision points identify the critical points where choice can have the greatest impact on outcomes. Additionally, experience can be a tremendous help toward increasing awareness of decision points. When clients reflect on the past guided by the helper, they can see examples of success and realize their strengths. Helpers can also assist the client to trace the decisions he/she has made and reflect on the results of those choices.

-o-

SECTION IV: ROLES AND PRACTICE CONTEXTS OF SOCIAL WORKERS

CHAPTER 11

LEARNING ACTIVITIES

Define the major social ills that social work addresses. Consider the value of promoting economic justice, mental alth, and civility.

WRITING ASSIGNMENT

Describe the client populations and client presenting problems that you wish to work with each day.

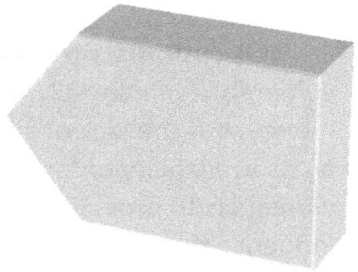

Chapter 11: Poverty, Health, and Institutions

Social workers around the world continue to wrestle with the challenges of poverty. Poverty is typically measured as an evaluation of subsistence, equity, and vulnerability.

Subsistence means having available the minimum, socially accepted requirements for wellbeing.

Equity measure refers to an assessment of the relative position (perceived and real-economic) of an individual or household in comparison with other individuals or households.

Vulnerability is the chance that an individual or household will be in poverty or some other unsustainable social circumstance.

It is customary to value subsistence, equity measures and vulnerability financially. Yet, poverty is felt not only in the lack of money, but the lack of access. Every healthy community is defined by its availability or lack of access. The social justice goal of social workers is to provide a clear voice for those without access and influence the definitions that undergird the allocation of assistance to those in need to promote informed access for all people.

Health is both a question of capacity to make choices and the awareness of all the choices that are possible. Empowerment in the context of health and wellbeing means creating a level playing field where each individual has the raw materials for success and access to the means of production. The needs may be different from person to person. Person A may require more resources than Person B to level the playing field and create the capacity to make informed choices.

Equity at the decision points means that the set of options and the perceived ability to access all options is equal for each person faced with the choice set. Person A may have previous experience that makes one choice more apparent than another which is obscured to Person B. Equity at the decision points reveals all choices to all persons. These are examples of the factors termed social determinants of health.

SOCIAL DETERMINANTS OF HEALTH

The World Health Organization defines **social determinants of health** as

"...conditions in which people are born, grow, live, work and age, including the health system...shaped by the distribution of money, power and resources at global, national and local levels."

The international organization has launched a commendable commission, sponsored a world conference, and provided overarching recommendations for reducing inequities in these conditions. Consider the WHO overarching recommendations:

- Improve daily living conditions
- Tackle the inequitable distribution of power, money, and resources
- Measure and understand the problem and assess the impact of action

Each of these recommendations is explained in further detail on the WHO site. A locally-applicable framework comprised of 3 considerations on which to structure institutional innovations and individual interventions may offer a practical translation of the WHO ideas. A translation begins with an alternate definition:

Social Determinants of Health are functions of a local community's governance of its Institutions, Environmental Factors, and Common Threads in Self-Governance.

Institutions

Humans engage in complex systems, even complex adaptive systems. Stated simply, people will not do better just because they know better or the opportunity is available. In order to address individual health, we will need to change the rules of the game rather than continually attempting to educate and appeal to the better nature of the players.

Institutions are the chess boards upon which each of us execute our lives. Institutions have an ability to force our behavior through a complex interaction between rules, social conformity, and individually created meaning. Local communities must measure and manage these institutions for the progress, justice and altruism supporting the health and wellbeing of citizens. Consider the primary institutions as follows: Faith, Family, Education, Entrepreneurship, and Health.

FAITH. Regardless of the diverse implementations of faith, they share a common expectation of a brighter future. Faith communities support citizens to believe in a future despite past failures or predictions based on the past. Consider that identified faith communities are a local community's first partners toward sustainable change.

FAMILY. The WHO gives primacy to the role of child development in the advancement of communities. Families provide the tools and techniques for evaluating relationships, social role definition, and work ethic. Local communities will do well to communicate a productivity focus supporting a family-level test bed for safe, sustainable risk and education that increases the potential for larger community success.

EDUCATION. Local communities must move beyond education as a simple requirement and provision of schools. They must offer insight into the process and mechanics of teaching, learning, and self-development integrating a new culture of creativity as an institutional innovation. Structure the process as a family interaction. Expand the interaction from child-centered to family-engaging. Re-envision education as a control system, and abandon the assembly-line model.

ENTREPRENEURSHIP. Expand the notion of employment, work, and wealth creation. It is important to engage and ensure fairness among employers. Also, local communities must, whether the employer base exists or not, promote the habits, perspective, and discipline that convert ideas into capital. Empower citizens to create products, connect to markets, and package individual expertise.

HEALTH. Expand the notion of health services to include the practice wisdom of the medical and mental health professions. Engage other institutions in education to structure health promoting environments and activities. The WHO supports exploration of the impact of environment, stress, nutrition. Local communities can effectively add relationship patterns, roles and affiliations, beauty and personal care (i.e. nail salons), and perceptions of self to the determinants of physical and mental development and holistic well-being.

Participation Factors

In order for institutions to flourish and achieve individual intervention, local communities will need to attend to the basic requirements of community participation: Housing, Transportation, Recreation, Emergency Services, and Safety (From Violence).

Housing is a basic provision of healthy communities. As the WHO recognizes, quality housing means clean water and sanitation. For local communities, it also means community spaces and integration with institutions. For example, in an eldercare independent living high rise, provide medical, college/certification, reunions, meditation, and inventor services in the building.

Transportation can be especially concerning in rural communities. Even in larger communities, transportation must involve a combination of private sector and public sector solutions. Examine the excess capacity and willingness to engage represented in institutions. For example, faith communities may be willing to run transportation services within certain communities if liability concerns could be worked out.

Recreation includes public spaces, but also private spaces. Local community planners would do well to engage with studies that support porches, outdoor gardens, terraces and patios. These structures support the health of the community (Evans & Wells, 2003). An example may be a competitive neighborhood grant sponsored by the local government in cooperation with a private sector home improvement store. The grant could propose to provide half of the funding needed to add a garden, a front porch, or re-pave sidewalk.

Emergency Services today is inextricably connected to disaster services in the minds of many citizens. Of course, a preparedness, triage, and contingency plan must be in place and market. Local communities will do well to also consider family, block, and neighborhood disaster planning support as well. Support these plans within the institutions rather than just printing brochures. For example, offer a community award for the school or faith community that registers or renews the most family emergency contact lists, fire escape plans, or other preparedness concerns.

Public safety does not always have to be active public safety interventions. Programs like community policing and "officer in residence" have not been reviewed to be panacea as a lone intervention. Yet, neighbors in such programs report a sense of safety. Moreover, officers in such arrangements report engaging with citizens in new and productive ways. Another idea may be connecting police professionals in homeowner's association or other community meetings to discuss strategies or citizen concerns.

Common Threads in Self-Governance (CTSG)

SGS is just a quick way to express that element of complex adaptive systems that motivates the individual to action. The adage suggests, "you can lead a horse to water, but you can't make it drink." Local governments can create institutions and environments that are fair, progressive, just, and altruistic, but this does not mean that those same principles are successfully communicated to the public. Certainly, even effective communication does not mean that the principles are adopted and practiced by the population.

Local communities can move another step toward effective communication of principles by transparently revealing knowledge system, mechanisms, relationships influencing choice models, and markets.

Knowledge System refers to the system of accreditation, credentialing, or authorization that both qualifies and licenses an individual or business to operate as an influencer within a community. Beyond the information that is typical with education, the knowledge system considers how authority is constructed. Without a knowledge of the individual's ability to garner authority, the motivation for any endeavor suffers. In other words, why try if you don't know if it will yield favorable results?

Mechanisms refer to the real processes of community progress. Essentially, it is community asset building as an institutional process ensuring access to information, relationships, and the means of production (e.g. co-ops, incubators, pre-screened health services, and more). Transparent sharing of mechanisms would result in a greater potential to match need, ideas, and personal assets with excess capacity, mentoring, and capital translation.

Relationships refer to a new way of providing information. Consider the decision points that an individual citizen considers along the process of action. As well, consider the social influences that attend every decision point. Build the information and social influence model into institutions and increase the potential for the individual citizen's choice to be influenced toward a more sustainable choice. For example, engage faith communities in health eating seminars including private sector businesses to cater events. Provide leaders with information on healthy diet and lifestyle knowing that these leaders influence citizens through lectures, modeling, after-service dinners, bake sales, and other events.

Markets refers to the core experience of complex systems. One event impacts the larger system in some way. Use marketing and public service channels as well as institutional information sharing (based on choice models) to regularly communicate the interrelatedness of citizens. For example, present a scenario in a public service announcement that tells the story of what results from one citizen neglecting to recycle or vaccinate. Focus the story on the impact of one citizen's choice on the available choice and well-being of other individual citizens.

ARNSTEIN'S LADDER

But what about instances when the client is not engaged in the discussion and therefore is not even cognizant of the decision points? For example, it is every person's right to vote in the United State, but some individuals do not exercise the right due to a real belief that one vote does not make a difference.

Social workers typically work in environments that seek to address deficits in access and promote equity. Social service environments based on deficit needs include: Substance Misuse and Addictions, Hospice & Palliative Care, Mental health, Developmental disabilities, Gentrification/Homelessness, Poverty, Foreclosure/Bankruptcy/Income Maintenance, Natural disaster/Crisis Intervention, and Corrections. But the question of equity at the decision points remains,

> "Do the assessments and interventions implemented by social workers provide age appropriate, informed, relational, real (understandable) equity at the decision points?"

And another question:

> What do social workers do to address the institutionalized and systematic denial of social justice through major barriers like classism, racism, sexism, ageism, homophobia, and anti-Semitism?

Arnstein's Ladder of Civic Participation speaks to the engagement of individuals in the decision making of communities. The ladder lists eight levels of increasing engagement organized in three clusters.

At the low end of engagement is **Non-participation**.

- Level 1 is Manipulation.
- Level 2 is Therapy.

In the moderate engagement is **Tokenism**.

- Level 3 is Informing.
- Level 4 is Consultation.
- Level 5 is Placation.

At the high end of engagement is **Citizen Power**.

- Level 6 is Partnership.
- Level 7 is Delegated Power.
- Level 8 is Citizen Control.

SUMMARY

Social workers must be about the business of individual change and social change. They must also operate at the high end of engagement in communities increasing Citizen Power as opposed to just manipulating and providing therapy.

Bibliographic Notes

The World Health Organization has done extensive work on social determinants of health. Explore recommendations at *who.int/social_determinants/en/*

For a primer on complex systems, see this BOHO Interactive video:
http://youtu.be/bN2N7gqAax0

.

Arnstein, Sherry R. "A Ladder of Citizen Participation," JAIP, Vol. 35, No. 4, July 1969, pp. 216-224.

Evans, G.W. and Wells, N.M. (2003). Housing and Mental Health: A Review of the Evidence and a Methodological and Conceptual Critique. Social Issues, 59(3). 475-500.

[WRITING EXAMPLE] The Truth about Altruism

Altruism is a not a concept that can be practiced without modification in professional social work. To fully sacrifice oneself for another person is unrealistic. It is important that social workers recognize the limits of altruism in their practices. Social workers do give of themselves, but not to the extent that their fitness, health, or well-being is compromised.

But, to discount the usefulness of altruism is to miss important points in the definition and application of the term. Biological altruism is where the action of an organism improves the fitness of another organism while reducing the fitness of the organism performing the act. This is only one definition. Common altruism, the type observed in human systems, is a cooperative interaction. This type of altruism may offer benefit to both the client and the social worker.

It is true that biological altruism does not fit the social work profession. Yet, a sense of altruism as mutual benefit or reciprocity is congruent with social work. In a reciprocal relationship, both parties give and receive something of value. When understood this way, it could be said that social work is a profession of altruists.

-o-

CHAPTER 12

LEARNING ACTIVITIES

:iculate the informal culture of the social
vork profession evident in the professional
roles, values, norms, and common
symbols. Reflect on the dual goal of social
work to facilitate individual change and
ial change.

WRITING ASSIGNMENT

Detail the social worker roles that you
the most comfortable with.

Chapter 12: Roles & Informal Professional Culture

The social workers mandate is client change AND social change. Client change is the requirement that each social worker assists in the coping and adaptation process of the client. Social change is the requirement that each social worker promote social justice in institutions and society for the well-being of individual clients and groups of clients.

Informally, social workers bring a set of roles to the helping process that, combined, are unique to the helping professions. The nine roles can be organized in four groupings: Direct services, Advocacy, Group services, and Administration.

DIRECT SERVICES groups two roles: Broker and Case Manager.

In the **Broker** role, social workers link clients with market resources. As a broker, the social worker must ensure the client's access to information about relationships and procedures. A beginning broker may be tempted to remain useful to the client by withholding information about connections and processes. In social work, the goal is to enable the client to eventually access needed markets without the help.

In the **Case Manager** role, social workers assist clients to cope with crises. As a case manager, the social worker must give the responsibility to the client in order to build self-sufficiency. The beginning case manager may be tempted to coddle the client supporting the client's dependency on the worker. Make no mistake, success means that the client builds her own system of supports.

ADVOCACY includes the roles of Initiator, Advocate, Mediator, and Negotiator.

In the **Initiator** role, social workers call attention to a need. Competence is a key attribute for the initiator. Competence results from doing your homework on the issues including cost analyses.

In the **Advocate** role, social workers represent the client against a more powerful entity. As an advocate, the social worker must balance her personal safety and professional integrity. Often, the role of advocate is assumed because inaction would violate the value of social justice.

In the **Mediator** role, social workers objectively resolve a conflict between two parties. As a mediator, the social worker must remain unbiased with no conflict of interests.

In the **Negotiator** role, social workers seek benefit on behalf of a client. As a negotiator, the social worker must be able to both advocate for the client and compromise with adversary.

GROUP SERVICES include a set of three roles: Organizer, Facilitator, and Educator.

In the **Organizer** role, social workers organize an activity or group. As an organizer, the social worker must balance the certainty of schedules with the spontaneity of creativity to produce the desired environment for the activity.

In the **Facilitator** role, social workers lead a group process. As a facilitator, the social worker seeks to ensure that the decisions and commitments made in the group process are accepted by the group and each member buys in to the decisions.

In the **Educator** role, social workers teach content to a client or group. As an educator, the social worker has the task to at once provide access and ease to the client while motivating the client's search for knowledge.

ADMINISTRATION as a grouping of social worker roles includes Evaluator and Administrator.

In the **Evaluator** role, social workers research and analyze the effectiveness of programs. As an evaluator, it is important that the social worker assess the program holistically for its value in addition to financial measures.

In the **Administrator** role, social workers manage toward a defined set of goals. As an administrator, the social worker must develop an approach that is not just managing but leading. Social workers are proactive agents. The social work administrator gets the best from her team and leads on the cutting edge of trends.

SOCIAL WORK ROLES

Role	Active Definition	Concern
Enabler	Assist client to cope with crisis.	Self-sufficiency or Dependency (Coddling)
Broker	Link client with resources	Access to Information or What I think You Should or Need to Know
Advocate	Represent the client against more powerful entity.	Personal safety and Professional Integrity
Initiator	Call attention to a need.	Competence and doing your homework
Mediator	Objectively resolve a conflict between two parties.	Unbiased, no conflict of interests.
Negotiator	Seeks benefit on behalf of a client.	Balance of client advocacy and compromise with adversary.
Facilitator	Leads a group process.	Outcomes accepted by the group as theirs.
Organizer	Organizes an activity or group.	Schedules versus creativity.

Educator	Teaches content to a client or group.	Providing access and motivating search for knowledge.
Evaluator	Researches and analyzes effectiveness.	Assessing holistic value not just money.
Administrator	Manages toward a defined set of goals.	Managing versus Leading.

[WRITING EXAMPLE] The Social Worker on Teams

Social workers are often called upon to work with inter-professional teams. In these instances, the professional training and value base of the professionals may be in conflict at times. It is important for the social worker to understand what her professional contribution is to the team. A clear role defined in cooperation with the team can be an important step toward group norming.

However, the social worker is always tasked with ensuring individual and social wellbeing in all his practice activities. Individual wellbeing refers to ensuring that the client's voice and wishes are always considered by the team. If at all possible, plans should be made in direct consultation with the client. In the absence of this, social workers may need to speak for the client.

Social wellbeing means that the social work is diligent in ensuring that barriers to client success in the system are removed. In addition, the social worker may need to educate the team to opportunities beyond the normal scope of practice experienced by other team members. As a professional that deals in social change, the social worker may have information or contacts in the community that the other professionals may be unaware of.

A clearly defined role created cooperatively with the inter-professional team is important to group norming. Yet, the social worker also must effectively incorporate her duty of individual change and social change for the wellbeing of the client. Inter-professional teams will not only benefit from the expertise represented in the social worker, the client will benefit most of all.

-o-

CHAPTER 13

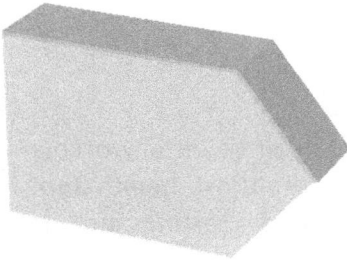

LEARNING ACTIVITIES

rticulate the formal culture of the social work profession, like settings, structure of client relationships, policy change, and research opportunities. Reflect on the value ocial work research.

WRITING ASSIGNMENT

Describe the practice contexts and work schedules that would satisfy you.

Chapter 13: Practice Contexts & Formal Professional Culture

Social workers address equity questions through a formal professional culture that

- seeks individual change in a multitude of Settings,
- advocates for just Policy, and
- builds competence through Research.

SETTINGS

Remember the social determinants of health? Social workers operate within a number of settings related to those health and well-being determinant factors and institutions. Settings include the following:

Family Settings

- Child Care
- Child Welfare
- Parent Services & Training

Faith Settings

- Churches
- Shelters
- YMCA

Business/Entrepreneurship Settings

- Not-For-Profit Agencies
- Private Practice & For-Profit Corporations

Health Settings

- Crisis Care & Other Emergency Medical Facilities
- Community Mental Health Agencies
- Neighborhood Clinics
- Mobile Health Services
- Nursing Homes

Education Settings

- Schools
- After School Settings
- Youth Crisis Centers

In addition, social workers work within many government offices including:

- Justice/Corrections Facilities
- Federal and State Government Programs
- Rural Services Providers

Job Titles for social workers vary. Typical job titles may be Case Manager, Clinician, Social Worker, Administrator, or Social Work Manager. Less Frequent titles could be Researcher, Politician, or Professor of Social Work. Alternate Titles could be Community Organizer, Advocate, Mediator, Behavioral Specialist, Program Coordinator, or Mental Health Specialist.

Social Workers have the opportunity to work with all people across the lifespan from Children to the Aged; all Socio-economics from upper-class through under-class; all geographic designations Local and International; and all Ecological Systems: individuals, families, groups, organizations, and communities.

POLICY

The concept of majority rule is a means to manage the complexity in situations of increased diffusion, membership, and history. By definition, majority rule creates a minority. It could be said that those who wish to oppress others deny them access to information, isolate people, and create barriers to markets. This is often achieved through the policies adopted by organizations and society.

The US Constitution provides a number of safeguards to guard against oppression of the minority by the majority. Examples include Individual Freedom (Article I (1) of the US Constitution), which states that individuals may choose any action unless the action hurts others. Equal Protection (Article XIV (14) of the US Constitution) ensures that laws apply to all citizens equally. Voting Rights (Article XIX (19) of the US Constitution) provides to all members with the right to vote.

Freedom of Speech (Article I (1) of the US Constitution) states that all members may contribute any idea to public debate. Individual property (Article V (5) of the US Constitution) ensures that member's property is not taken without just compensation. Due Process (Article XIV (14) of the US Constitution) ensures that disputes concerning member's rights are resolved fairly.

Social workers promote policies that ensure equity through access to Information--ensuring that diverse voices are present and allowed to operate; Access to People--ensuring collaboration among the diverse parties is promoted and provided space; and, Access to Markets--ensuring that individuals are supported toward sustaining innovations they create and learning from failed innovations.

RESEARCH

Evidence-Based Practice is a reasoned approach to practice leading to scientific experimentation. Social workers, like other helping professionals, seek to do what has been proven to work for clients.

The social work code of ethics admonishes social workers to contribute to the knowledge base of the profession and continue the research cycle, which is to Practice, Document, Hypothesize, Experiment, Script New Models of Practice, and repeat.

Social work researchers employ the same scientific method used in other sciences and apply it to behavioral science. Social work researchers

- identify a problem,
- collect information about the problem,
- create a goal to solve the problem,
- set up an intervention to address the problem,
- evaluate the results in comparison to prior functioning, and
- communicate the results.

The results of social work research are structure for application in a way that establishes best practices with the goal of improved service to clients. The best practices are packaged and disseminated across the profession with the goal of creating shared expertise and supporting data-based decision making.

[WRITING EXAMPLE] The Social Worker as Researcher

Research may be the most important of the social worker tasks. Research provides a knowledge base for social work including evidence-based practices that demonstrate the effectiveness of interventions. Without social research, program evaluation, and practice evaluation, there would be no evidence of the good that social workers do. Without research, it would be difficult to train new social workers as well.

Yet, research alone is no panacea. Research has to be disseminated and consumed. It has to be applied in real-life situations. Research would be immaterial without the practice that is applied each day in social service, non-profit, faith-based, private practices and other settings.

The real value is evident when research and practice meet, when research is informed by practice and practice is informed by research. This relationship creates a cycle that promises to improve services to clients. Best practices based on evidence can become the standard taught to new social workers. Those social workers continually evaluate their practice to contribute new knowledge to the profession.

-o-

www.ingramcontent.com/pod-product-compliance
Lightning Source LLC
Chambersburg PA
CBHW030655270326
41929CB00007B/379